Whuppity Stoorie

RETOLD by **John Warren Stewig**

illustrated by
Preston McDaniels

holiday house / New York

Library of Congress Cataloging-in-Publication Data
Stewig, John W.
Whuppity Stoorie / retold by John Warren Stewig;
illustrated by Preston McDaniels.—1st ed.
p. cm.
Summary: In order to cure
her ailing pig, a Scottish widow agrees
to give a strange woman whatever she wants
and then the widow must guess the woman's name
or give up her baby.
ISBN 0-8234-1749-2
[1. Folklore—Scotland.] I. McDaniels, Preston, ill. Title.
PZ8.1.W8574 Wh 2003
398.2'09417'02—dc21
[E]   2002038717

In honor of all strong Scottish women
who protected their ingenuity
J. W. S.

For Cindy, Abby, and Liz
with deepest love and respect
P. M.

Listen closely, my bairns, for a story about the goodwife o' Kittlerumpit. Come sit ye down and listen well while I tell you how the goodwife bested one o' the fairy folk.

Now, the goodman o' Kittlerumpit was a wandering sort o' body, and he went to the fair one day, and not only never came home again but never more was heard of. When the goodman o' Kittlerumpit was gone, the goodwife was left ill provided for. Little money had she, and a wee bairn, Robert, to look after besides. Everybody was sorry for her, but nobody helped her, which was a common case. However, the goodwife had a sow, and that was her only consolation, for the sow was soon to farrow and she hoped for a good litter o' wee piglets.

One day the wife went to the sty to fill the sow's trough, and what did she find but the sow lying on her back, grunting and groaning, flailing her trotters, ready to leave this world for the next.

This was a new blow to the goodwife's heart, so she sat down beside the pen with the bairn on her knee and wept sorrier than ever she did for the loss o' her goodman.

The cottage was built on a brae with a fir forest behind it. When the goodwife was wiping her eyes, she chanced to look down the hill, and what did she see but an old woman, coming slowly up the road. She was dressed in green, with a short white apron, and a black velvet hood, and a steeple-crowned beaver hat on her head. She had a walking staff as long as herself in her hand—the sort o' staff that old men and old women helped themselves with in times long gone.

When the goodwife saw the green gentlewoman near her, she rose and made a curtsy.

"Madam," quoth she, "I'm one o' the most misfortunate women alive."

"I dinna wish to hear old news and idle gossip, goodwife," responded the woman. "I know ye've lost your goodman—the fingers o' hard times pinch us all now and again. I know o' your sow's sorry state. Now, what will you give me if I cure her?"

"Anything your ladyship likes," replied the witless woman, never guessing what she had to deal with.

"Let's seal the bargain by wetting our thumbs," said the lady in green. So thumbs were wet and into the sty madam marched, her skirts swirling like a spring wind over the peat bog.

She scowled long at the sow and then began to mutter to herself what the goodwife couldn't well understand, but she told me it sounded like

Pitter, patter,
holy water.

Then she took out o' her pooch a wee bottle, with something like oil in it, and rubbed the sow above the snoot, ahind the ears, and on the tip o' the tail.

"Get up, beast," she commanded. No sooner said than done. Up bangs the sow with a grunt, and away to the trough for her slops.

The goodwife o' Kittlerumpit was joyful now and would have kissed the very hem o' the green madam's gown-tail, but the madam wouldn't let her.

"I'm not so fond o' fine manners," she said, "but now that I have righted your sick beast, let us end our bargain. You'll not find me an unreasonable greedy body. I always like to do a good turn for a small reward. All I ask, and will have, is baby Robert on your bosom."

The goodwife o' Kittlerumpit knew now who she was facing, and gives a scream like a stuck pig. The green woman was a fairy, no doubt. So she prays, and weeps, and begs, and scolds, but nothing would do any good.

"Spare me your din," says the fairy, "screaming as if I was as deaf as a doornail. But this I'll let you know—I cannot, by the law we live under, take your bairn until the third day after this; and not then, if ye can tell me my right name." So madam swirls her skirts round behind the swine sty, and the goodwife falls down in a faint behind the horse trough.

The goodwife o' Kittlerumpit could sleep none that night for weeping and all the next day the same, cuddlin' Robert till she near squeezed his breath out. But the second day she thinks o' taking a walk in the wood I told ye of, to ease her mind. So, with the bairn in her arms, she set out. She went far in among the trees, where there was an old quarry hole grown over with weeds, and a bonny spring well in the middle o' it. Before she came very nigh she heard the whirring o' a spinning wheel, and a voice lilting a song. So the wife crept quietly among the bushes and peeped over the brow o' the quarry, and what did she see but the green fairy striving at her wheel and singing loud enough to wake the dead.

"Little knows our good dame at home,
That Whuppity Stoorie is my name!"

Aha, thought the wife. I've gotten the way to outwit the madam at last. So she went home far lighter than she came out, as ye may guess, laughing like a madcap with the thought o' besting the old green fairy.

Ye must know now, bairns, that this goodwife was a jovial woman, and aye merry when her heart wasn't sorely overladen. So she thinks to have some sport with the fairy. At the appointed time she puts the bairn behind the pigpen and sits down on it herself. Then she pulls her cap over her left ear, crooks her mouth on the side, as if she were weeping, and a filthy face she made, ye may be sure. She hadn't long to wait, for up the hill mounts the green fairy, neither lame nor lazy.

Long before she got near the pigpen, she cries out: "Goodwife o' Kittlerumpit, ye well know what I come for. Stand and deliver." The wife pretends to weep sorrier than before, and wrings her hands, and falls on her knees, crying, "Och, sweet madam mistress, spare my only bairn and take the weary sow."

"The devil take the sow for my share," quoth the fairy. "I come not here for swine's flesh. Don't be perverse, hizzie, but give me the child instantly."

"Oh, dear lady mine," replied the weeping goodwife, "forbear my poor bairn and take myself."

"The devil's in thee, self-willed woman," said the fairy, looking like storm clouds gathering over the moor. "I'll say you're clean demented. Who in all the earthly world, with half an eye in their head, would ever meddle with the likes o' thee?"

I know this made the goodwife o' Kittlerumpit bristle, for though she had two bleary eyes, and a long red nose besides, she thought herself as bonny as the best o' the ladies who dance at the fair. So she bangs off her knees, sets up her cap, and with her two hands folded afore her, she makes a curtsy down to the ground.

"Dear lady," she says, "you promised I could guess your name, to repay my debt. Do I guess your name to be Esmanderelda?"

The green woman rocked back on her heels and laughed at the futile guess.

"If that's not right, then perhaps it is Fernandora?" asked the goodwife.

Once again the magical fairy laughed, rather rudely, at the guess.

"I' troth, fair madam," quoth the goodwife, "I might have had the wit to know that the likes o' me is not fit to tie the shoestring o' the high and mighty princess Whuppity Stoorie!"

If a fluff of gunpowder had come out o' the ground, it couldn't have caused the fairy to leap higher than she did.

Then down she came again, dump on her shoe heels, and whirling round, she ran down the hill, screeching for rage, like an owl chasing with the witches.

The goodwife o' Kittlerumpit laughed till she was like to cry. Then she took up Robert and went into her house, singing the entire way:

"A good day's work, my bonny wee tyke,
You're ready for your feeding;
Whuppity Stoorie has run away,
And happiness we're seeking."

So now, bairns, ye know what happens to those who get themselves crosswise with one o' the fairies, who always have mischief in mind when they help us humans. Stay shy o' them and solve your own problems.

Children, naturally curious, are often intrigued by guessing, so I thought this tale would intrigue them. In the tale the goodwife must guess the green fairy's name to avoid losing her child. This guessing motif relates the tale to versions of *Rumpelstiltskin* (as in Paul Zelinsky's retelling, Dutton 1986) and to Margot Zemach's *Duffy and the Devil* (Farrar 1973) as well as to *Tom Tit Tot* by Evaline Ness (Scribner's 1965).

Here it is not a dwarf, a devil, "that," or indeed a little "manikin" as in Arthur Rackham's *Grimm's Fairy Tales* (SeaStar 2001) but rather a magical healing fairy woman whose name must be guessed.

In preparing my retelling, I consulted early versions, such as the one found in *The Scottish Fairy Book* by Elizabeth W. Grierson (Lippincot 1910), in which the reteller included several sentences identifying the location of Kittlerumpit as somewhere "in the neighborhood of the Debateable Land, which is as all the world knows, on the Borders." Versions such as this describe the conflicts between the British and Scottish—historic information that doesn't speak to children today—so I eliminated such details.

Some of the versions I consulted required extensive translating, as the language used contained many unfamiliar terms. Though published recently, both David Buchan's *Scottish Tradition* (Routledge 1984) and Neil Philip's *The Penguin Book of Scottish Folktales* (Penguin 1995) are really only accessible to adults with patience to use the glossary Buchan provides to decipher the story. Words such as *anent* (concerning), *kemping* (striving), and *contramawcious* (obstinate) are charmingly archaic but must be simplified in a retelling for young listeners.

In most of the versions I found of "Whuppity Stourie," the goodwife guesses only once. But since things often happen in threes in tales such as this, one of the changes I made was to insert two false tries before she reveals that she does in fact know the name of her helpful but devious guest.

There are few other versions of this tale available to children today. Kathleen Ragan's version, in *Fearless Girls, Wise Women and Beloved Sisters* (Norton 1998), is a straightforward retelling that explains the goodwife's poverty by disposing of the husband, as I did in my retelling. There's little Scottish dialect in this variant, and the goodwife reveals that she knows the name immediately, not after two false tries, as in my retelling.

In Carolyn White's picture book version, *Whuppity Stoorie* (Putnam 1997), there is no new baby. Rather, White makes the goodwife's resourceful daughter, Kate, able to solve the problem. This version is particularly noteworthy for the imaginatively elaborated language, including naming the pig and the new litter.